KU-671-379

READINGS
IN SICKNESS

Compiled by Norman Autton

London SPCK

First published 1976
SPCK
Holy Trinity Church
Marylebone Road
London NW1 4DU

Printed in Great Britain by
Bocardo & Church Army Press Ltd, Oxford

ISBN 0 281 02923 7

Contents

The cry of earth's anguish went up unto God,
   'Lord, take away pain!
   The shadow that darkens the world Thou hast made;
   The close coiling chain
   That strangles the heart; the burden that weighs
   On the wings that would soar.
   Lord take away pain from the world Thou hast made,
   That it loves Thee the more!'

Then answered the Lord to the world He had made:
   'Shall I take away pain;
   And with it the power of the soul to endure,
   Made strong by the strain?
   Shall I take away pity, that knits heart to heart,
   And sacrifice high?
   Will you lose all your heroes that lift from the flame
   White brows to the sky?
   Shall I take away love that redeems with a price,
   And smiles through the loss?
   Can ye spare from the lives that would climb unto mine,
   The Christ on His Cross?'

C. L. DRAWBRIDGE

Acknowledgements

Thanks are due to the following for permission to reproduce material of which they are the publishers, authors, or copyright owners:

Metropolitan Anthony of Sourozh

BBC Publications

The Bodley Head

The Burrswood Herald

Church in Wales Publications

The Churches' Council for Health and Healing

The Most Reverend Donald Coggan

Wm. Collins Sons & Co. Ltd

Constable & Co. Ltd

The Daily Telegraph

Darton, Longman & Todd Ltd

The English Province of the Order of Preachers
(Trustees of the Vann Estate)

The Expository Times

Gill & Macmillan Ltd

William Heinemann Ltd

Hodder & Stoughton Ltd

Longman Group Ltd

Macmillan, London and Basingstoke

Mayhew-McCrimmon Ltd, Great Wakering, Essex

Methodist Publishing House (Epworth Press)

A. R. Mowbray & Co. Ltd

Miss Ruth Pitter

Routledge & Kegan Paul Ltd

The Saint Andrew Press

Search Press Ltd

S.C.M. Press Ltd

Mrs Frances Temple

Trustees of the Tagore Estate

Extract on p. 68 reprinted by permission from C. S. Lewis, *Letters to an American Lady*, edited by Clyde S. Kilby, Copyright © 1967 by Wm. B. Eerdmans Publishing Co.

The Authorized Version of the Bible is Crown copyright; extracts used herein are by permission.

Extracts from the New English Bible, second edition © 1970, are used by permission of Oxford and Cambridge University Presses.

Thanks are due to the following for permission to reproduce material of which they hold the American rights:

Doubleday & Co. Inc.: J. Neville Ward, *Five for Sorrow, Ten for Joy*

Harcourt Brace Jovanovich Inc.: *The Secret of the Golden Flower*, tr. R. Wilhelm, Commentary by C. G. Jung, English tr. C. F. Baynes

Macmillan Publishing Co. Inc. (New York): Ivan Turgenev, *Dream Tales and Prose Poems*, tr. Constance Garnett

Simon & Schuster Inc.: Joshua Loth Liebman, *Peace of Mind* (Canadian rights also)

The Sterling Lord Agency Inc.: Norton Juster, *The Phantom Tollbooth*, © 1961 by Norton Juster, published in America and Canada by Random House Inc. (Canadian rights also).

Introduction

Whenever you are ill at home or in hospital the average day seems to be long. You are often awake early in the morning, and the remainder of the day is apt to hang heavily. It is not easy to adjust to a period of bed-rest, particularly if you normally live a very busy life. Much will depend on how you react to such circumstances. You can either lie in your bed and brood, full of self-pity and introspection, or you can take advantage of this time of rest and quiet to think and reflect.

This little bedside anthology of readings offers a selection of readings and Scripture references which can be used in times of stillness and silence—for example, when you are lying awake in the early morning or preparing for your rest period in the afternoon, when you feel lonely or depressed, or last thing at night before the lights go out.

Sickness is not a time for lengthy concentration, and you will soon find it is extremely difficult to read for long periods. (This is one reason why a paperback book, short stories, and anthologies are such popular bedside literature.) Besides the inevitable state of physical and mental weakness which makes it well-nigh impossible for the mind to dwell on one topic for any length of time, there are the constant interruptions, the frequent comings and goings, of a busy hospital ward. For this reason the following selections of readings have been chosen as much for their brevity as for their content.

The extracts have been culled from a variety of writings which deal with subjects of hope and healing, prayer and penitence, praise and thanksgiving in sickness. A number of them have been written by those who themselves have undergone much suffering in their lives, for it is only those who have been sore tested and tried who can best help those who are undergoing their test now.

For love's strength standeth in love's sacrifices;
And whoso suffers most hath most to give.

Each passage should be read slowly, meaningfully, meditatively, and as far as possible made to relate to the present situation. A single sentence or phrase from a reading might profitably be used as an 'affirmation' or 'arrow-head' prayer during times of pain, or during a sleepless night. Should you sometimes be too tired or weak to look up a passage yourself, do ask your friends, visitors, or your hospital chaplain to read it for you. In this way the extract can be shared and become a corporate rather than a personal act.

It is the hope of the compiler that the thoughts contained in the following pages may help to support and encourage you. When full advantage is taken of such periods of sickness, and the negative is transferred into the positive, many patients leave sick-room or hospital not only physically the stronger but spiritually the healthier. Please God it may be so with you.

NORMAN AUTTON

24 *February* 1975
St Matthias Ap.

The School of Sickness

I am sure that we have need to learn not only in the school of health but also in the school of sickness. These breaks in life, and the sense of helplessness and weakness which attend them, are not simply periods to be 'got over'—to be made the best of till we can 'start again'—but they have a meaning which we can find, if we only look with the eye of faith. It is strange how, although God sees the whole way in which we ought to go, He leaves us in comparative darkness. We need, I am sure, revelation. 'Lord, open the young man's eyes, that he may see.' We shall take the wrong turning if we trust to our ordinary eyes; we shall find the path if we have the eye of faith to see what God is revealing.

FORBES ROBINSON

Therefore, my brothers, I implore you by God's mercy to offer your very selves to him: a living sacrifice, dedicated and fit for his acceptance, the worship offered by mind and heart. Adapt yourselves no longer to the pattern of this present world, but let your minds be remade and your whole nature thus transformed. Then you will be able to discern the will of God, and to know what is good, acceptable, and perfect.

ROMANS 12.1–2

A Lay-by

You may have been in bed only since yesterday, or for some time already. But however these things may be in your particular case, all those who are in bed have this in common: they have got something wrong with them. That is the reason why they are laid by.

A lay-by on the road is a place where the tired driver can pull in and rest. . . . he can think about his journey to this point and that which lies ahead. That done, he and his engine will both leave the lay-by better for their stay. Your present lay-by in bed offers similar constructive opportunities for your whole self, and it is most important that you should recognise and make the most of them. But probably you have already read as much as you feel fit for at the moment. So we suggest that at this point you shut this book, and make this affirmation, lying with closed eyes: God loves me. GOD . . . LOVES . . . ME. Say that repeatedly. It is a fact.

A RELIGIOUS OF C.S.M.V.

Thus we have come to know and believe the love which God has for us.

God is love; he who dwells in love is dwelling in God, and God in him. . . . There is no room for fear in love; perfect love banishes fear. For fear brings with it the pains of judgement, and anyone who is afraid has not attained to love in its perfection. We love because he loved us first.

1 JOHN 4.16, 18–19

Beginning the Day

Begin the day by offering it and yourself to God. Look at the day as an individual thing that begins and ends with completeness in itself; then take this thing, this day, and offer it to God to be a day for His use . . . The day at once becomes a unity and life becomes unified. However many distracting details come into the day, both mind and emotions are dominated, not by them but by the sense that you have only one thing to do—namely, to act in obedience to God with regard to them.

GEORGE S. STEWART

Listen to my words, O Lord,
consider my inmost thoughts;
heed my cry for help, my king and my God.
In the morning, when I say my prayers,
thou wilt hear me.
I set out my morning sacrifice
and watch for thee, O Lord.

PSALM 5.1–3

Redeeming the Time

In a long illness the counting up of resources however small, from the point of view of their positive use, will often bring all kinds of good results. You have been given a 'present' of time, something all too rare and often envied in these bustling days. How can you best use it? . . . Can you read some good literature to nourish your mind or comfort your soul? Can you listen to some good music, good plays or talks, church services or other religious broadcasts?

What about personal relationships? Is there any upset or broken relationship which you might do something about? Can you make the best use of the opportunities of getting to know and understand your doctors, nurses, fellow patients, visitors (including your minister) and wardmaids a little better, and give out your friendliness and encouragements . . . This may help them in ways beyond your imagination. Aren't all these much better and more helpful than crying over spilt milk?

WILLIAM L. CARRINGTON

Be most careful then how you conduct yourselves: like sensible men, not like simpletons. Use the present opportunity to the full . . . let the Holy Spirit fill you: speak to one another in psalms, hymns, and songs; sing and make music in your hearts to the Lord; and in the name of our Lord Jesus Christ give thanks every day for everything to our God and Father.

EPHESIANS 5.15–16, 18–20

Rest and Recollection

What a bore that you are still parked in hospital . . . Our dear Lord will teach you much while you are so close to Him in pain of body and weariness of soul—your little Gethsemane. Don't distress yourself or argue with yourself and don't worry too much about the details of your prayers. Now you must rely upon the prayers of the Church on earth and in heaven. Just try to hold the hand of the Lord Jesus. Your prayer may well be only: 'I want to love Thee—look deep into my heart and see that desire there—hold me up in the times of pain, darkness and rebellion, they are not my true self and I want to be good for Thy sake.' Don't for goodness sake try to relate your sufferings to your sins . . . Of course talk with Our Lord about it all in your own way and do what the Psalmist says, 'Complain unto the Lord.' Ask questions, provided you allow Our Lord to answer them—which means silence in the heart and some recollection. 'Be of good cheer, in the world ye shall have tribulation, in me ye shall have Peace.' Don't fret; rest in the Lord.

RAYMOND RAYNES

I cry aloud to the Lord;
to the Lord I plead aloud for mercy.
I pour out my complaint before him
and tell over my troubles in his presence.
When my spirit is faint within me,
thou art there to watch over my steps.

PSALM 142.1–3

The Good Patient

The people, be they doctors, nurses, friends, or relatives, who do things for and to you, are helping you to bear the burden of your illness. In illness there is always danger lest, in one's own distress, one should forget that one is not the only pebble on the beach or patient in the ward, and grow demanding. The good patient, on the other hand, will take none of these ministries for granted, but be grateful for each thing, each time. In doing that you keep the law of Christ entire. For when you take your nurse's services, for instance, humbly and gratefully, and not as yours by right, you help her bear the burden of her life and work. The opportunities for doing this are countless, and there is no telling how blest and how far-reaching the effect may be, if they are taken.

A RELIGIOUS OF C.S.M.V.

What thanks can we return to God for you? What thanks for all the joy you have brought us, making us rejoice before our God while we pray most earnestly night and day to be allowed to see you again and to mend your faith where it falls short? . . . and may the Lord make your love mount and overflow towards one another and towards all, as our love does towards you.

1 THESSALONIANS 3.9–10, 12

My Neighbour

I saw myself, in dream, a youth, almost a boy, in a low-pitched wooden church. . . . All at once some man came up from behind and stood beside me. I did not turn towards him; but at once I felt that this man was Christ. Emotion, curiosity, awe overmastered me suddenly. I made an effort . . . and looked at my neighbour.

A face like everyone's, a face like all men's faces. The eyes looked a little upwards, quietly and intently. The lips closed, but not compressed; the upper lip, as it were, resting on the lower; a small beard parted in two. The hands folded and still. And the clothes on him like every one's.

'What sort of Christ is this?' I thought. 'Such an ordinary, ordinary man! It can't be!'

I turned away. But . . . I felt again that it really was none other than Christ standing beside me.

And suddenly my heart sank, and I came to myself. Only then I realised that just such a face—a face like all men's faces is the face of Christ.

TURGENEV

God be gracious to us and bless us,
God make his face shine upon us,
that his ways may be known on earth
and his saving power among all the nations.
Let the people praise thee, O God;
let all peoples praise thee.

PSALM 67.1–3

Why This Waste?

The horrible thing about much of our suffering is that it seems so futile. What good does it do—this unchosen, undesired, stupid, useless pain?—It need not be futile: that is my comfort. It can be, and a thousand times it is, an inspiration. To whom do you turn, when it is your turn to suffer? To one who suffers or has suffered—no one else can help you . . . If I want help in bearing pain, I find it in the hope that I am taking my share in the world's pain. I cannot choose it, not being very brave, but I can accept it in that way—endurance of pain is part of the price to be paid for lifting the world out of the jungle and the morass into which it has fallen.

MAUDE ROYDEN

Jesus was at Bethany in the house of Simon the leper, when a woman came to him with a small bottle of fragrant oil, very costly; and as he sat at table she began to pour it over his head. The disciples were indignant when they saw it. 'Why this waste?' they said; 'it could have been sold for a good sum and the money given to the poor.' Jesus was aware of this, and said to them, 'Why must you make trouble for the woman? It is a fine thing she has done for me. You have the poor among you always; but you will not always have me. . . . I tell you this: wherever in all the world this gospel is proclaimed, what she has done will be told as her memorial.'

MATTHEW 26.6–11, 13

Why, Lord?

Lord, suffering disturbs me, oppresses me.
I don't understand why you allow it.
Why, Lord? . . .
Suffering is odious and frightens me . . .
Son, it is not I, your God, who has willed suffering, it is
  men.
But I came, and I took all your suffering upon me, as I took
  all your sins,
I took them and suffered them before you.
I transformed them, I made of them a treasure.
They are an evil, but an evil with a purpose,
For through your sufferings, I accomplish redemption.

MICHEL QUOIST

'Now my soul is in turmoil, and what am I to say? Father,
save me from this hour. No, it was for this that I came to
this hour. Father, glorify thy name.' A voice sounded from
heaven: 'I have glorified it, and I will glorify it again.' . . .
[Jesus said,] 'Now is the hour of judgement for this world;
now shall the Prince of this world be driven out. And I shall
draw all men to myself, when I am lifted up from the earth.'
This he said to indicate the kind of death he was to die.

JOHN 12.27–8, 31–3

9

How, Not Why

Jesus did not escape from suffering, nor do we. But he took it and made something wonderful of it. He transformed it; and through his wounds mankind is healed. His love in the midst of his suffering changed the meaning of events, made the ugly things beautiful and the hard things acceptable. Two pieces of wood became the symbol of salvation; a crown of thorns his halo; Golgotha his throne of glory.

Let me put it this way. When suffering hits us, it is natural enough to ask the question 'Why?' Jesus did. But it is more important to ask the question 'How? How will God make this thing, which to me is so negative, into a plus in his hands? Is it possible that I am on my back so that I may learn to look up?' That might be the most wonderful thing I could do.

DONALD COGGAN

. . . we know that he who raised the Lord Jesus to life will with Jesus raise us too, and bring us to his presence . . . No wonder we do not lose heart! Though our outward humanity is in decay, yet day by day we are inwardly renewed. Our troubles are slight and short-lived; and their outcome an eternal glory which outweighs them far. Meanwhile our eyes are fixed, not on the things that are seen, but on the things that are unseen: for what is seen passes away; what is unseen is eternal.

2 CORINTHINIANS 4.14, 16–18

God's Will be Done

We have got into a habit of saying, 'God's will be done' in a mood of resignation. That is blasphemous. It means that, having found we cannot have our own way, we are ready to put up with His as second best. It will not do. We ought to say 'Thy will be done' in ungovernable hope, knowing it to be so much better than our own. . . . It is the prayer you should want to offer if you loved God with all your heart, and you may learn to love Him with all your heart if you realise what this prayer means, and try to enter into it. Never let it become for you a formula.

WILLIAM TEMPLE

We can approach God with confidence for this reason: if we make requests which accord with his will he listens to us; and if we know that our requests are heard, we know also that the things we ask for are ours. . . . We know that the Son of God has come and given us understanding to know him who is real; indeed we are in him who is real, since we are in his Son Jesus Christ. This is the true God, this is eternal life.

I JOHN 5.14–15, 20

Help to Endure

Lord, now I am ill I have plenty of time to pray, but I am too taken up with my pain and fears to do more than say, please help me to endure, don't leave me, and remember me when I become so concerned with myself that I forget you. Help me to put myself in your hands even though all I want to do is to complain and resent the suffering.

MICHAEL HOLLINGS AND ETTA GULLICK

Here is the proof that we dwell in him and he dwells in us; he has imparted his Spirit to us. Moreover, we have seen for ourselves, and we attest, that the Father sent the Son to be the saviour of the world, and if a man acknowledges that Jesus is the Son of God, God dwells in him and he dwells in God. Thus we have come to know and believe the love which God has for us.

God is love; he who dwells in love is dwelling in God, and God in him.

1 JOHN 4.13–16

Daily 'Readings'

That daily quarter of an hour, for now forty years or more, I am sure has been one of the greatest sustenances and sources of calm for my life. Of course, such 'reading' is hardly reading in the ordinary sense of the word at all. As well could you call the letting a very slowly dissolving lozenge melt imperceptibly in your mouth 'eating'. Such reading is, of course, meant as directly as possible to feed the heart, to fortify the will—to put these into contact with God—thus, by the book, to get away from the book to the realities it suggests—the longer the better . . . During such reading we are out simply and solely to feed our own poor soul, such as it is '*hic et nunc*'.

BARON VON HÜGEL

For all the ancient scriptures were written for our own instruction, in order that through the encouragement they give us we may maintain our hope with fortitude. And may God, the source of all fortitude and all encouragement, grant that you may agree with one another after the manner of Christ Jesus, so that with one mind and one voice you may praise the God and Father of our Lord Jesus Christ.

ROMANS 15.4–6

13

Lord, Teach Us to Pray

In sickness the days and nights seem long; the slow hours drag on in weariness. But the time would seem short and the hours full of interest if we could learn the lesson of intercession. Begin by praying for some of your fellow-sufferers by name. You can sympathize with them now with an intenser sympathy than you had when in health. Then go on to intercede for doctors and nurses and all who minister to the sick, especially those who minister to you. Think of the Christ-like work of medical missions ... Perhaps one day you will be able to thank God for this time of sickness, because in it you have found His answer to the cry of every sincere Christian, 'Lord, teach us to pray.'

ARTHUR W. HOPKINSON

And it came to pass, that, as he was praying in a certain place, when he ceased, one of his disciples said unto him, Lord, teach us to pray, as John also taught his disciples.

And he said unto them, When ye pray, say, Our Father which art in heaven, Hallowed be thy name. Thy kingdom come. Thy will be done, as in heaven, so in earth.

Give us day by day our daily bread.

And forgive us our sins; for we also forgive every one that is indebted to us. And lead us not into temptation; but deliver us from evil.

LUKE 11.1-4 A.V.

Praying As We Can

The best and greatest thing we can do is to pray. We must pray 'as we can and not as we can't', it is true, but when we are praying in a critical situation we soon find out that our prayer does not consist in the words we use; the fewer they are, the better. Our Lord's prayer in the Garden was an affair of His whole being, but the actual words He used were few and short; but they said everything. 'Short prayer pierceth heaven.' Simply to say over and over again 'My God . . .' may be the most real and the most profound prayer we have ever offered in our lives.

OLIVE WYON

Jesus then came with his disciples to a place called Gethsemane . . . He went on a little, fell on his face in prayer, and said, 'My Father, if it is possible, let this cup pass me by. Yet not as I will, but as thou wilt.' . . . He went away a second time, and prayed: 'My Father, if it is not possible for this cup to pass me by without my drinking it, thy will be done.' . . . So he left them and went away again; and he prayed the third time, using the same words as before.

MATTHEW 26.36, 39, 42, 44

Praying for Courage

Suppose we are going to pray for courage. We can begin with an act of adoration of the courageous Christ upon the Cross, and pray that we may have courage such as that. We pray for courage for ourselves or our friend. Then our whole prayer seeks to be an act of communication with that courage, a courageous going forth to Him, accepting whatever suffering is to come and seeking communion with Him, bringing all our powers of endurance and courageous choice into communion with Him who chose to go to Calvary for us all. Then, as it were, holding the pierced hand and going forth into life, we seek to meet whatever we have to meet in co-operation with Him. We shall not lose our tranquility, we shall not lose our temper, if we are quietly going with our Lord all the way.

FATHER ANDREW

Finally then, find your strength in the Lord, in his mighty power. Put on all the armour which God provides, so that you may be able to stand firm against the devices of the devil. . . . Therefore, take up God's armour; then you will be able to stand your ground when things are at their worst, to complete every task and still to stand. Stand firm, I say.

EPHESIANS 6.10–11, 13

Distractions

There may, of course, be occasions when you have to face just deadness and distractions, especially if you are tired. Remember always that God's presence in your soul does not depend on whether you feel it or not. He is there just the same, and only deliberate sin can drive him away. You have to learn sooner or later pure faith, that is, holding on to that presence of God, to the fact of God, when everything within you seems dead and cold, and perhaps only distractions. That state has been compared with our Lord asleep in the boat (in the soul) with his disciples. The storm arises, and the temptation is to get worried and distracted and try to wake him up (as it were) instead of keeping still and as recollected as possible, waiting for him to make the first move.

HUBERT NORTHCOTT

That day, in the evening, he said to them, 'Let us cross over to the other side of the lake.' . . . A heavy squall came on and the waves broke over the boat until it was all but swamped. Now he was in the stern asleep on a cushion; they roused him and said, 'Master, we are sinking! Do you not care?' He awoke, rebuked the wind, and said to the sea, 'Hush! Be still!' The wind dropped and there was a dead calm.

MARK 4.35, 37–9

Fellowship with Christ

The world is full of pain today; each of us has a share; for some it is a slight burden, for others it is crushing. But every Christian can turn it into a blessing if he will seek the companionship of Christ in his suffering; then the pain becomes a new point of fellowship with Christ; and even our suffering becomes part of the price of the world's redemption as we fill up what is left over of the suffering of Christ.

Pain does not then cease to be pain; but it ceases to be barren pain; and with fellowship with Christ upon the Cross we find new strength for bearing it and even making it the means by which our hearts are more fully cleansed of selfishness and grow towards perfect love.

WILLIAM TEMPLE

All I care for is to know Christ, to experience the power of his resurrection, and to share his sufferings, in growing conformity with his death, if only I may finally arrive at the resurrection from the dead. It is not to be thought that I have already achieved all this. I have not yet reached perfection, but I press on, hoping to take hold of that for which Christ once took hold of me.

PHILIPPIANS 3.10–12

In Pain

Pain—most real pain, which comes ready to our hand for turning into right pain—gets offered us by God. Try more and more at the moment itself, without any delay or evasion, without any fixed form, as simply, as spontaneously as possible, to cry out to God, to Christ our Lord, in any way that comes most handy, and the more variously the better . . . 'Oh, may this pang deepen me, may it help to make me real, real—really humble, really loving, really ready to live or die with my soul in Thy hands' . . . And so on, and so on. You could end by such ejaculations costing your brain practically nothing. The all-important point is, to make them at the time and with the pain well mixed up into the prayer.

BARON VON HÜGEL

For ours is not a high priest unable to sympathize with our weaknesses, but one who, because of his likeness to us, has been tested every way, only without sin. Let us therefore boldly approach the throne of our gracious God, where we may receive mercy and in his grace find timely help.

HEBREWS 4.15–16

In Continuing Pain

Until now we have been thinking in terms of healing, but what of the times when there seems to be only pain and when there is humanly speaking no healing to be found? Even out of a situation like that great things can come. When Leighton, the Scottish divine, was in all his pain, he said: 'I have learned more of God since I came to this bed than ever I did before.' It is then that so many have found it true and in all their afflictions he was afflicted (Isaiah 63.9), and that when they passed through the waters God was with them (Isaiah 43.2). In that Jesus Christ himself was tested and tried, he can help others who are going through it.

WILLIAM BARCLAY

It was clearly fitting that God for whom and through whom all things exist should, in bringing many sons to glory, make the leader who delivers them perfect through sufferings. . . . The children of a family share the same flesh and blood; and so he too shared ours, so that through death he might break the power of him who had death at his command, that is, the devil . . . For since he himself has passed through the test of suffering, he is able to help those who are meeting their test now.

HEBREWS 2.10, 14, 18

Mental Pain

The twisted body cannot easily be hidden. The abnormal mind is more amenable to such treatment. Mental pain is far more common than many would suppose. The mind is such a delicate instrument that we can suffer a thousand agonies of fear and yet be living apparently normal lives. The problem for most of us is how to cope with this abnormality and pain . . . It is a source of hope if we can believe that God gave us life to live to the full, and that he makes this fullness more and more possible . . . sufferers from mental pain have within them the principle of hope which they can use to minister to their own need for healing. Try it yourself. You have a great fear. Go down into this fear, with your hand in Christ's, and find out all about it through him, and you will emerge again on the way to victory. Use your vicar or minister to help you farther on the way.

NORMAN W. GOODACRE

As a hind longs for the running streams,
so do I long for thee, O God.
. . .
How deep I am sunk in misery,
groaning in my distress;
yet I will wait for God;
I will praise him continually,
my deliverer, my God.

. . .
The Lord makes his unfailing love shine forth
alike by day and night;
his praise on my lips is a prayer
to the God of my life.

PSALM 42.1, 5, 8

Bearing Pain

I remember Archbishop William Temple in one of his books
writing that if you pray for any particular virtue, whether
it be patience or courage or love, one of the answers God
gives to you is an opportunity for exercising that virtue . . .
Long hours of ignoble pain were a severe test. In the middle
of that torture they asked me if I still believed in God.
When, by God's help I said, 'I do,' they asked me why
God did not save me, and by the help of his Holy Spirit,
I said, 'God does save me. He does not save me by freeing
me from pain or punishment, but he saves me by giving me
the spirit to bear it.'

LEONARD WILSON

In the same way the Spirit comes to the aid of our weakness.
We do not even know how we ought to pray, but through
our inarticulate groans the Spirit himself is pleading for us,
and God who searches our inmost being knows what the
Spirit means, because he pleads for God's people in God's
own way; and in everything, as we know, he co-operates for
good with those who love God and are called according to
his purpose.

ROMANS 8.26-8

Fortitude

Give me that tranquil courage which is content to await your gift. I live by what comes to me from you. . . . Sometimes my need and exhaustion seem very great, and you seem very silent: surrounding conditions seem very stony, and hard. Those are the moments when my faith is purified, when I am given my chance of patience and fortitude and tranquillity: abiding among the stones in the wilderness and learning the perfection of dependence on you.

EVELYN UNDERHILL

. . . for God himself has said, 'I will never leave you or desert you'; and so we can take courage and say, 'The Lord is my helper, I will not fear; what can man do to me?' . . . Jesus Christ is the same yesterday, today, and for ever.

HEBREWS 13.5–6, 8

The True Function of Suffering

How wonderful it is, is it not, that literally only Christianity has taught us the true peace and function of suffering. The Stoics tried the hopeless little game of denying its objective reality, or of declaring it a good in itself (which it never is), and the Pessimists attempted to revel in it, as a food to their melancholy, and as something that can no more be transformed than it can be avoided or explained. But Christ came, and He did not really explain it; He did far more, He met it, willed it, transformed it, and He taught us how to do all this, or rather He Himself does it within us, if we do not hinder the all-healing hands.

BARON VON HÜGEL

Let your bearing towards one another arise out of your life in Christ Jesus. . . . Bearing the human likeness, revealed in human shape, he humbled himself, and in obedience accepted even death—death on a cross. Therefore God raised him to the heights and bestowed on him the name above all names, that at the name of Jesus every knee should bow—in heaven, on earth, and in the depths—and every tongue confess, 'Jesus Christ is Lord', to the glory of God the Father.

PHILIPPIANS 2.5, 8–11

The Sound of Silence

Milo walked slowly down the long hall and into the little room where the Soundkeeper sat listening intently to an enormous radio set, whose switches, dials, knobs, meters, and speakers covered one whole wall, and which at the moment was playing nothing.

'Isn't that lovely?' she sighed. 'It's my favourite programme—fifteen minutes of silence—and after that there's a half-hour of quiet and then an interlude of lull. Why, did you know that there are almost as many kinds of stillness as there are of sounds? But, sadly enough, no one pays any attention to them these days.'

NORTON JUSTER

'Peace is my parting gift to you, my own peace, such as the world cannot give. Set your troubled hearts at rest, and banish your fears. You heard me say, "I am going away, and coming back to you." If you loved me you would have been glad to hear that I was going to the Father; for the Father is greater than I. I have told you now, beforehand, so that when it happens you may have faith.

'I shall not talk much longer with you, for the Prince of this world approaches. He has no rights over me; but the world must be shown that I love the Father, and do exactly as he commands; so up, let us go forward!'

JOHN 14.27–31

The Silence of Jesus

The silence of Jesus on the Cross is the greatest silence of all. Many people fear and hate silence; and most of us have times when to wait in silence seems the hardest thing we have ever had to do. If we are waiting for a fateful decision, or watching someone suffer, it is terrible to feel that we are 'doing nothing'. Yet here, where God is most at work, He seems to be doing nothing. . . . But all this time—what was He doing? There He hung, helpless, fastened hand and foot to the wood of the cross; He had given Himself entirely into the hands of men; in the eyes of men He was defenceless; He was at their mercy. And yet, in reality: 'the Cross is the great act of God. On it Christ does nothing. The soldiers and the crowds were the people who did things' . . . and what things! Jesus could not move. He 'could not do anything, except redeem the world'. This is how God works, behind a thick veil.

OLIVE WYON

Jesus was now brought before the Governor; and as he stood there the Governor asked him, 'Are you the king of the Jews?' 'The words are yours', said Jesus; and to the charges laid against him by the chief priests and elders he made no reply. Then Pilate said to him, 'Do you not hear all this evidence that is brought against you?'; but he still refused to answer one word, to the Governor's great astonishment.

MATTHEW 27.11–14

When Tired

It is a good plan, when tired, to learn to pray sitting quiet and relaxed, letting our Lord take hold and keep you in his peace, filling you with his healing power. It can be wonderfully refreshing and deepen your sense of communion with him, who is Light and Life and Love. Meanwhile you can make little acts of faith and love and thanksgiving and adoration, or just repeat his name. It is a great step forward in our spiritual life to learn our own utter weakness and the reality of his power and love. The cross comes to us but it is in the power of the Risen Lord alone that we can bear it.

HUBERT NORTHCOTT

Do you not know, have you not heard?
The Lord, the everlasting God, creator of the wide world,
grows neither weary nor faint;
no man can fathom his understanding.
He gives vigour to the weary,
new strength to the exhausted.
Young men may grow weary and faint,
even in their prime they may stumble and fall;
but those who look to the Lord will win new strength,
they will grow wings like eagles;
they will run and not be weary,
they will march on and never grow faint.

ISAIAH 40.28–31

Suffering in Christ

My best help when pain comes, or any specially depressing time, is to remember as clearly as I can that by God's mercy and grace I am a member of Christ, and that to suffer is not to suffer alone, but to suffer in Christ, and that the Christ in me deigns to share my sufferings. 'The fellowship of the sufferings of Christ.' It makes a great difference to remember that. And to remember that our Lord makes the suffering of those who suffer as His members contribute blessings to others, to 'His Body the Church.' 'I fill up that which is behind in the sufferings of Christ, for His Body's sake, the Church.'

FATHER CONGREVE

. . . the Spirit of God joins with our spirit in testifying that we are God's children; and if children, then heirs. We are God's heirs and Christ's fellow-heirs, if we share his sufferings now in order to share his splendour hereafter. For I reckon that the sufferings we now endure bear no comparison with the splendour, as yet unrevealed, which is in store for us.

ROMANS 8.16–18

The Healing Cross

There are times when the mind is beyond the reach of any theory, however true. Deep suffering cannot be expressed in words; it cannot be reached by words. The sight of Jesus on the Cross and His silence help here. For it is God Himself that people want when they are touching the deepest things in life. And nowhere do they find Him so near, so healing, so understanding, as on the Cross . . . He does not meet them with words, or with explanations; but He takes them into His keeping, and they are at peace.

OLIVE WYON

Yet on himself he bore our sufferings,
our torments he endured,
while we counted him smitten by God,
struck down by disease and misery;
but he was pierced for our transgressions,
tortured for our iniquities;
the chastisement he bore is health for us
and by his scourging we are healed.

ISAIAH 53.4–5

Victory through Mastery

At the end, just before He died, He cried out, 'My God, My God, why hast thou forsaken me?'

As with Jesus, so with us, there is no escape from the human situations in which we find ourselves. God will not say, 'Abracadabra', and get us out of it. Nor will He supply us with a spiritual drug to deaden whatever doubt or anxiety or fear or pain may come our way, and cheer us up so that we feel good. Perhaps we confuse escape with something quite different: victory. For Jesus there was no escape. But there was victory . . .

The victory consisted precisely in not running away, in not trying to escape . . . And by thus facing and accepting what came to Him from outside and from within, without lessening the agony, He mastered it. He made it into His servant. He used it as the way of surrender, of giving all.

H. A. WILLIAMS

From midday a darkness fell over the whole land, which lasted until three in the afternoon; and about three Jesus cried aloud, *'Eli, Eli, lema sabachthani?'*, which means, 'My God, my God, why hast thou forsaken me?' . . . Jesus again gave a loud cry, and breathed his last . . . There was an earthquake . . . And when the centurion and his men who were keeping watch over Jesus saw the earthquake and all that was happening, they were filled with awe, and they said, 'Truly this man was a son of God.'

MATTHEW 27.45-6, 50, 52, 54

One Day at a Time

In the realm of bearing, what has to be borne has to be borne now. We never have to bear today what we shall have to bear tomorrow. It is not God's will that we play neurotic games with the future and try to feel now the weight of burden not yet laid on us. If we knew the future, how dark it may be, we might lose heart. If we knew the future, how bright it is, we might relax that tension in our concern about our present duty that means we put our utmost into it. So God's will for us concerns what he wants us to do in the present. All he asks us to bear is only for now, and he offers sufficient power for this assignment. If we add to it the thought of tomorrow's evil we shall fail.

J. NEVILLE WARD

'Therefore I bid you put away anxious thoughts . . . Set your mind on God's kingdom and his justice before everything else, and all the rest will come to you as well. So do not be anxious about tomorrow; tomorrow will look after itself. Each day has troubles enough of its own.'

MATTHEW 6.25, 33–4

Lift Up Your Hearts

He requires no great matters of us; a little remembrance of Him from time to time, a little adoration; sometimes to pray for His grace, sometimes to offer Him your sufferings, and sometimes to return Him thanks for the favours He has given you, and still gives you, in the midst of your troubles, and to console yourself with Him the oftenest you can. Lift up your heart to Him, sometimes even at your meals, and when you are in company: the least little remembrance will always be acceptable to Him. You need not cry very loud; He is nearer to us than we are aware of.

BROTHER LAWRENCE

'. . . if it is at all possible for you, take pity upon us and help us.' 'If it is possible!' said Jesus. 'Everything is possible to one who has faith.' 'I have faith . . . help me where faith falls short.'

MARK 9.22–4

Joy in Adversity

Strangely, joy often speaks most eloquently in adversity . . .
Jesus does not deny that life can be a crucifixion. He asserts
that it is not waste . . . The last cry from the Cross is a cry
of joy. It was not sudden release from pain, but a declaration
that pain is not pointless, that the ingredients of this poison
can be made medicinal. Yet not easily. Suffering can be met
with resentment and then is wasted. Or it can be received
and its malice removed. Then it is made redemptive. The
sweetest smile may be that which lights the face of the
sufferer. It has strength and a kind of nobility. It has joy . . .

Calvary is a slope all are called to climb and Jesus pioneers
the path. The end is not death but life, and this revealing is
the ground of Christian joy. This joy keeps a man on the
march. There is a spring in his step and a light in his eye
for a man passed this way before. He suffered and he cried
in his agony. It was a cry of joy.

HUGH LAVERY

And what of ourselves? . . . we must throw off every encum-
brance, every sin to which we cling, and run with resolution
the race for which we are entered, our eyes fixed on Jesus,
on whom faith depends from start to finish: Jesus who, for
the sake of the joy that lay ahead of him, endured the cross,
making light of its disgrace, and has taken his seat at the
right hand of the throne of God.

HEBREWS 12.1–2

Helping Others

In entrusting us with a load of pain God is often giving us a power to help others greater than that possessed by the most eloquent of preachers or the wisest of teachers. To carry with us that which automatically brings out the best side of other people, that which sends them away with fresh courage and renewed cheerfulness, that which brings them nearer to each other, and to goodness, and therefore to God, what more lovely ministry could any of us desire?

G. E. CHILDS

For the same God who said, 'Out of darkness let light shine', has caused his light to shine within us, to give the light of revelation—the revelation of the glory of God in the face of Jesus Christ.

We are no better than pots of earthenware to contain this treasure, and this proves that such transcendent power does not come from us, but is God's alone. Hard-pressed on every side, we are never hemmed in; bewildered, we are never at our wits' end; hunted, we are never abandoned to our fate; struck down, we are not left to die. Wherever we go we carry death with us in our body, the death that Jesus died, that in this body also life may reveal itself, the life that Jesus lives.

2 CORINTHIANS 4.6–10

Inner Strength

Let me not pray to be sheltered from dangers but to be fearless in facing them.

Let me not beg for the stilling of my pain but for the heart to conquer it.

Let me not look for allies in life's battlefield but to my own strength.

Let me not crave in anxious fear to be saved but hope for the patience to win my freedom.

Grant me that I may not be a coward, feeling your mercy in my success alone; but let me find the grasp of your hand in my failure.

RABINDRANATH TAGORE

The Lord is my light and my salvation;
whom should I fear?
The Lord is the refuge of my life;
of whom then should I go in dread?
. . .
For he will keep me safe beneath his roof
in the day of misfortune;
he will hide me under the cover of his tent;
he will raise me beyond reach of distress.

. . .

Wait for the Lord; be strong, take courage,
and wait for the Lord.

PSALM 27.1, 5, 14

Supernatural Strength

I am a poor creature indeed compared with the Christian
martyrs, but I did have some very severe pain myself once.
The doctor was quite apologetic. It was a thing they would
so gladly spare the patient, he said, if they could; but so far
they hadn't found any way to do so. But afterwards I
wondered if it wasn't better to have the pain. There was
such astonishment in it, for one thing. It was Experience
with a capital E. I thought, 'Nobody knows anything who
hasn't had a pain like that.' It quite altered my character
for a bit; I felt miraculously enlightened, and I had so much
more moral courage. . . . To me, it was a tiny sample of the
way in which the martyrs are placed beyond life's ordinary
concerns and given some kind of supernatural strength.

RUTH PITTER

Fear nothing, for I am with you;
be not afraid, for I am your God.
I strengthen you, I help you,
I support you with my victorious right hand.

ISAIAH 41.10

Being Receptive

I always thought that, when we accept things, they over-power us in one way or another. Now this is not true at all, and it is only by accepting them that one can define an attitude toward them. So now I intend playing the game of life, being receptive to whatever comes to me, good and bad, sun and shadow that are for ever shifting, and, in this way, also accepting my own nature with its positive and negative sides. Thus everything becomes more alive to me. What a fool I was! How I tried to force everything to go according to my idea!

A PATIENT'S LETTER TO JUNG

I waited, waited for the Lord,
he bent down to me and heard my cry.
He brought me up out of the muddy pit,
out of the mire and the clay;
he set my feet on a rock
and gave me a firm footing;
and on my lips he put a new song,
a song of praise to our God.
Many when they see will be filled with awe
and will learn to trust in the Lord:
happy is the man
who makes the Lord his trust.

PSALM 40.1–4

The Love of God

Love is giving, and true happiness is a great love coupled with much serving. The daily service of a hospital ward— a doctor's rounds,—a heart of courage,—a father's tenderness,—a mother's arms,—who handles them holds holy things, belonging to us all. . . .

Are you saying, 'But what of the innumerable millions of innocent suffering people—millions of them all over the world?' I know. But the God I know does not love and help upon the scale of millions. He loves, and helps, comforts and saves upon the scale of one.

He said not,

> Thou shalt not be tempested,
> Thou shalt not be travailed,
> Thou shalt not be afflicted.

But he said,

> Thou shalt not be overcome.

THE DISTRICT NURSE

'Then the king will say to those on his right hand, "You have my Father's blessing; come, enter and possess the kingdom that has been ready for you since the world was made. For when I was hungry, you gave me food; when thirsty, you gave me drink; . . . when I was ill you came to my help" . . . Then the righteous will reply, "Lord, when was it that we saw you hungry and fed you, or thirsty and gave you drink . . . When did we see you ill . . . and come to visit you?" And the king will answer, "I tell you this: anything you did for one of my brothers here, however humble, you did for me." '

MATTHEW 25.34–40

We Shall Overcome

'We Shall Overcome' is a watchword made famous by Dr. Martin Luther King in his crusade for equitable conditions for negroes. It is an echo of St. John's Epistle . . . In our individual experience the conflict persists and we can have no real peace within except through victory. We shall overcome: and, in a sense which can be turned from metaphor into experienced reality, we have overcome, because we are 'in Christ' by faith. In the Gospel of John we read that Jesus said to His disciples just before His crucifixion: 'These things have I spoken unto you that in me ye may have peace. In the world ye have tribulation; but be of good cheer; I have overcome the world.'

W. R. MATTHEWS

. . . every child of God is victor over the godless world. The victory that defeats the world is our faith, for who is victor over the world but he who believes that Jesus is the Son of God? . . . that God has given us eternal life, and that this life is found in his Son. He who possesses the Son has life indeed; he who does not possess the Son of God has not that life.

I JOHN 5.4–5, 11–12

Contentment

There is a story in the Tales of Hasidim by Martin Buber which tells of a Rabbi who lived in utter dereliction—in hunger and thirst, in cold and loneliness, but who recited every day the eighteen blessings and the eighteen benedictions. One day someone said to him, 'How can you be so hypocritical. God has given you nothing and yet you thank Him for all His gifts.' The Rabbi replied: 'You do not understand. God looked at me and thought, what does this man need to be fulfilled, to become what he is capable of becoming? He needs hunger and cold and loneliness and these He has given me in such abundance that I rejoice in His generosity.'

METROPOLITAN ANTHONY OF SOUROZH

. . . I have learned to find resources in myself whatever my circumstances. I know what it is to be brought low, and I know what it is to have plenty. I have been very thoroughly initiated into the human lot with all its ups and downs—fullness and hunger, plenty and want. I have strength for anything through him who gives me power. But it was kind of you to share the burden of my troubles.

PHILIPPIANS 4.11–14

Inner Growth

A famous sculptor who wished to tell us that sometimes the inner part of us grows stronger as the outward part grows weak, put it like this: 'The more the marble wastes, the more the statue grows.' God does not send sickness, but He uses it. We can glorify God in time of sickness. We need not wait for our bodies to be healed before we do that. Offer Him yourself, your sickness, your pain. Think about those words used of your Lord, 'Made perfect through suffering.' Pray that through suffering you may grow more like Him. Very peacefully and happily rest your weakness on His divine Strength.

T. W. CRAFER

He that dwelleth in the secret place of the most High shall abide under the shadow of the Almighty.
I will say of the Lord, He is my refuge and my fortress: my God; in him will I trust.
Surely he shall deliver thee from the snare of the fowler, and from the noisome pestilence.
He shall cover thee with his feathers, and under his wings shalt thou trust: his truth shall be thy shield and buckler.

PSALM 91.1–4 A.V.

Willing Acceptance

Submission is a passive, negative thing that implies resignation and even resentment. But active, willing, conscious acceptance of our share in the tragedy of life, this is something positive and creative . . . If you are prepared to face pain in this way, accepting it and believing that it can be turned to practical use, you can make a strange discovery. Not only do you find out the way to bear it so that it hurts you less; you know that in its willing acceptance there lie ways of growth in personality and sympathy and enrichment of life which before you never suspected. There are few things more inspiring than the sight of a great misfortune cheerfully and heroically borne; and it is in the manner of its acceptance that there lies the key. It is not the suffering but the way it is borne which ennobles.

LEONARD WILSON

Praise be to the God and Father of our Lord Jesus Christ, the all-merciful Father, the God whose consolation never fails us! He comforts us in all our troubles, so that we in turn may be able to comfort others in any trouble of theirs and to share with them the consolation we ourselves receive from God.

2 CORINTHIANS 1.3–4

The Christian Community

Any community of Christians will have a concern for all its members. When any member is ill, the others will rally round in sympathy and helpfulness. There will be believing and persistent prayer, calling God's love to the aid of those in trouble, so much greater and more effective than our own . . . Living in Christ's way will enable us to share in Christ's health, and make available to us the abundant life of spirit, mind and body which is God's will for all.

GEORGE APPLETON

If one organ suffers, they all suffer together. If one flourishes, they all rejoice together.

Now you are Christ's body, and each of you a limb or organ of it. Within our community God has appointed, in the first place apostles, in the second place prophets, thirdly teachers; then miracle-workers, then those who have gifts of healing, or ability to help others or power to guide them, or the gift of ecstatic utterance of various kinds.

1 CORINTHIANS 12.26–8

Members of a Family

We are a family: we suffer because of one another, and also, unconsciously, we suffer for one another . . . We are all a family; in a true sense we are each responsible for all. Of Christ it was said that for our sake he was made sin; and we too in our turn are meant to share the sin and sorrow of the world in union with him, that out of that sharing the sin and sorrow may be healed. Perhaps the problem of evil and pain can never be wholly solved; but evil and pain can be resolved: the darkness can be transformed into light. It is to that we are called.

GERALD VANN

Christ was innocent of sin, and yet for our sake God made him one with the sinfulness of men, so that in him we might be made one with the goodness of God himself. . . . God's own words are:

In the hour of my favour I gave heed to you;
on the day of deliverance I came to your aid.

The hour of favour has now come; now, I say, has the day of deliverance dawned.

2 CORINTHIANS 5.21, 6.2

Loneliness

You are never really alone, although no one is near you. When you seem most alone God is with you: not out there, not up there, but within the depths of your being, in your very solitariness . . . In the emptiness, in the silence of solitude, yes, and in the desolation of loneliness, there God is to be found . . .

In the solitude Jesus was there—'he went up into a mountain apart to pray; and when the evening was come, he was there alone.' Jesus not only shared our solitude but he shared too a terrible burden of loneliness. Abandoned by his friends, forsaken even by the God in whom he had always trusted, he spoke what are surely the loneliest words that have ever been uttered: 'My God, my God, why hast thou forsaken me?' The last word on loneliness is that it has been shared by God Incarnate.

Hugh Montefiore

'If you love me you will obey my commands; and I will ask the Father, and he will give you another to be your Advocate, who will be with you for ever—the Spirit of truth. The world cannot receive him, because the world neither sees nor knows him; but you know him, because he dwells with you and is in you. I will not leave you bereft; I am coming back to you.'

John 14.15–17

More than Conquerors

As there are some men to whom the things that should have been for their wealth are, indeed, an occasion of falling, so are there others to whom the things that might have been for their hindrance are an occasion of rising; 'who going through the vale of misery use it for a well, and the pools are filled with water.' And 'they shall go from strength to strength'—in all things more than conquerors through Him Who loveth them; wresting out of the very difficulties of life a more acceptable and glorious sacrifice to lift to Him; welcoming and sanctifying the very hindrances that beset them as the conditions of that part which they, perhaps, alone can bear in the perfecting of His saints, in the edifying of the Body of Christ.

FRANCIS PAGET

. . . and yet, in spite of all, overwhelming victory is ours through him who loved us. For I am convinced that there is nothing in death or life, in the realm of spirits or super-human powers, in the world as it is or the world as it shall be, in the forces of the universe, in heights or depths—nothing in all creation that can separate us from the love of God in Christ Jesus our Lord.

ROMANS 8.37–9

The Grace of Gratitude

Sickness teaches us the blessing of health. For how many years of health have you to give thanks? Sickness teaches us the blessing of friendship. How thankful we should be for the kindness and sympathy, perhaps the undeserved kindness and sympathy, of our friends. What a true blessing is the skill of doctors, the patience of nurses, and all the wonderful ministry of healing in a Christian country. Many people have learned the grace of gratitude for the first time on a bed of pain.

ARTHUR W. HOPKINSON

As he was entering a village he was met by ten men with leprosy. . . . One of them, finding himself cured, turned back praising God aloud. He threw himself down at Jesus's feet and thanked him. And he was a Samaritan. At this Jesus said: 'Were not all ten cleansed? The other nine, where are they? Could none be found to come back and give praise to God except this foreigner?' And he said to the man, 'Stand up and go on your way; your faith has cured you.'

LUKE 17.12, 15–19

Thank You, Lord

Lord, it's not easy to understand suffering. I rebel at it in myself and in others. But I've met a man who has been suffering intensely for years. I sat by his bed and he almost writhed in pain—and he was cheerful and full of hope, and he said: 'How good God is!' Well, Lord, who am I to complain then? Thank you for the lesson, Lord.

MICHAEL HOLLINGS AND ETTA GULLICK

O Lord, it is good to give thee thanks,
to sing psalms to thy name, O Most High,
to declare thy love in the morning
and thy constancy every night.
. . .
How great are thy deeds, O Lord!
How fathomless thy thoughts!

PSALM 92.1–2, 5

Losing Faith

You know that weakness of body often seems to lead to weakness of spirit. We seem to be slipping away from God. Our hold on faith grows feeble. We want to make an effort of faith and prayer, but all effort seems impossible. At such times Christ will give us His own message of comfort. 'My strength is made perfect in weakness.' The more we realize our own weakness the more God is willing to reveal His strength. God comes to us; there is no need for us to go to Him. It is not effort that is required, but quiet waiting upon God.

ARTHUR W. HOPKINSON

Peter called to him: 'Lord, if it is you, tell me to come to you over the water.' 'Come', said Jesus. Peter stepped down from the boat, and walked over the water towards Jesus. But when he saw the strength of the gale he was seized with fear; and beginning to sink, he cried, 'Save me, Lord.' Jesus at once reached out and caught hold of him, and said, 'Why did you hesitate? How little faith you have!' They then climbed into the boat; and the wind dropped. And the men in the boat fell at his feet, exclaiming, 'Truly you are the Son of God.'

MATTHEW 14. 28–33

A Sense of Humour

We all have a tendency to use the right end of the telescope in looking at our own troubles and the wrong end in looking at the troubles of others. For this reason we are apt to increase our own burden by magnifying small details in our daily life till they become a grievous load to carry. There is no greater solvent for such exaggeration than humour . . . laughter separates the essential from the unessential, and when the chaff has blown away the grain will be left. St. Teresa, after long experience of the sisters in her charge, was inspired to add to the litany an extra clause: 'From all silly devotions Good Lord deliver us'; and we might well follow her example and pray to be delivered from all silly worries by the grace of humour.

REGINALD SOMERSET WARD

'You are light for all the world. A town that stands on a hill cannot be hidden. When a lamp is lit, it is not put under the meal-tub, but on the lamp-stand, where it gives light to everyone in the house. And you, like the lamp, must shed light among your fellows, so that, when they see the good you do, they may give praise to your Father in heaven.'

MATTHEW 5.14–16

The Present Moment

The present moment is delicate; handle it with care. It provides only a narrow passage; there's no room for worry. It passes quickly, and so it won't tire you out. It is a moment pregnant with possibility, but you have to give it direction and meaning. It alone possesses reality and it alone provides an arena for action. Its opportunities are limitless, for in it we meet the God of love. Don't shoulder the burden of the past, refuse to give any consideration to the future simply out of fear: that'd be the prompting of cowardice. Don't brood over the past, refuse to be frightened by the prospect of the future, confidently abandon yourself to God: that's the prompting of love. God is awaiting you in the present moment.

MICHEL QUOIST

All I can say is this: forgetting what is behind me, and reaching out for that which lies ahead, I press towards the goal to win the prize which is God's call to the life above, in Christ Jesus.

Let us then keep to this way of thinking, those of us who are mature. If there is any point on which you think differently, this also God will make plain to you. Only let our conduct be consistent with the level we have already reached.

PHILIPPIANS 3.13–16

Strength in Weakness

Our Lord must have experienced this feeling of separation a thousand-fold. He was one with His Father; throughout His life on earth we know that He was in constant communion with Him. How unbelievable it must have seemed to Him. How can we compare our moments of dereliction with those He endured? He was sinless, there was no question of His deserving what was happening to Him.

But the desolation passed and He was able to say at last 'Into Thy hands I commend my Spirit'. He was with His Father again and God grant that it may always be the same with us, and that we may be enabled to echo His words.

When these words are said, then gradually the agony will lessen, and by God's grace we shall be able to see that what seemed to be unbearable can through Him become able to be borne.

'Thy strength is sufficient for my weakness.'

'E.B.'

'My grace is all you need; power comes to its full strength in weakness.' I shall therefore prefer to find my joy and pride in the very things that are my weakness; and then the power of Christ will come and rest upon me. Hence I am well content, for Christ's sake, with weakness, contempt, persecution, hardship, and frustration; for when I am weak, then I am strong.

2 CORINTHIANS 12.9–10

Waiting . . . Waiting

You have the waiting—waiting till the X-rays are developed and till the specialist has completed his observations. And while you wait, you still have to go on living—if only one could go underground, hibernate, sleep it out . . . And one prays; but mainly such prayers as are themselves a form of anguish.

Some people feel guilty about their anxieties and regard them as a defect of faith. I don't agree at all. They are afflictions, not sins. Like all afflictions, they are, if we can so take them, our share in the Passion of Christ. For the beginning of the Passion—the first move, so to speak—is in Gethsemane.

C. S. LEWIS

Then he went out and made his way as usual to the Mount of Olives, accompanied by the disciples. When he reached the place he said to them, 'Pray that you may be spared the hour of testing.' He himself withdrew from them about a stone's throw, knelt down, and began to pray: 'Father, if it be thy will, take this cup away from me. Yet not my will but thine be done.'

And now there appeared to him an angel from heaven bringing him strength, and in anguish of spirit he prayed the more urgently; and his sweat was like clots of blood falling to the ground.

LUKE 22.39–44

Patience

Impatience and irritability very often attack us. God allows such things to happen to test the quality of our love and humility. It is the little sudden things that catch us off our guard. So we have to be watchful and always positive—aiming at love and patience and glad to have opportunities of showing them. 'Watch and pray', said our Lord, 'that ye enter not into temptation.' It will come, but we need not enter into it. It isn't temptation if one doesn't even feel it; but one need not give way to the feeling. So don't be distressed if sometimes you feel it; but don't let it get hold of you.

HUBERT NORTHCOTT

We ask God that you may receive from him all wisdom and spiritual understanding for full insight into his will, so that your manner of life may be worthy of the Lord and entirely pleasing to him. We pray that you may bear fruit in active goodness of every kind, and grow in the knowledge of God. May he strengthen you, in his glorious might, with ample power to meet whatever comes with fortitude, patience, and joy.

COLOSSIANS 1.9–11

54

Before an Operation

Perhaps the most difficult time will be the period before we receive our pre-medication, and we are screened off. At this time loneliness can engulf us and fear overcome us, yet the privacy and the peace can be welcome and provide us with an atmosphere of tranquillity for thought and prayer. We can use 'affirmations' such as 'Into thy hands I commend my spirit': 'I will fear no evil for thou art with me'. . . We can pray for those who will be ministering to us, and in turn we ourselves become conscious of being uplifted and supported by the prayers of the Church. Gradually we shall drift off into sleep, freed from all fear, cared for by skilled doctors and nurses of the theatre team, supported by the grace of the sacraments and sustained by the power of prayer.

NORMAN AUTTON

The Lord is my shepherd; I shall want nothing.
He makes me lie down in green pastures,
and leads me beside the waters of peace;
he renews life within me,
and for his name's sake guides me in the right path.
Even though I walk through a valley dark as death
I fear no evil, for thou art with me,
thy staff and thy crook are my comfort.

PSALM 23.1–4

Penitence

It is penitence which creates intimacy with our Lord. No one can know Him intimately who has not realised the sickness of his own soul and obtained healing from the physician of souls. Our virtues do not bring us near to Christ—the gulf between them and His holiness remains unbridgeable. Our science does not bring us near to Him, nor our art. Our pain may give us a taste of fellowship with Him, but it is only a taste unless the great creator of intimacy —penitence—is also there. . . .

Let us come with our hearts ready to respond to that shining forth of the Love of God. Let us see how we look in that presence. Then let us acknowledge our unfitness to be near Him, and hear Him say in answer: 'Today shalt thou be with Me.'

WILLIAM TEMPLE

If we claim to be sinless, we are self-deceived and strangers to the truth. If we confess our sins, he is just, and may be trusted to forgive our sins and cleanse us from every kind of wrong; but if we say we have committed no sin, we make him out to be a liar, and then his word has no place in us.

1 JOHN 1.8–10

Peace of Mind

Once, as a young man full of exuberant fancy, I undertook to draw up a catalogue of the acknowledged 'goods' of life . . . I set down my inventory of earthly desirables: health, love, beauty, talent, power, riches and fame—together with several minor ingredients of what I considered man's perfect portion.

When my inventory was completed I proudly showed it to a wise elder who had been the mentor and spiritual model of my youth . . . 'This,' I told him confidently, 'is the sum of mortal goods. Could a man possess them all, he would be as a god.'

At the corners of my friend's old eyes, I saw wrinkles of amusement gathering in a patient net. 'An excellent list,' he said, pondering it thoughtfully. . . . 'But, you have forgotten the one ingredient lacking which each possession becomes a hideous torment'. . . 'And what,' I asked, peppering my voice with truculence, 'is that missing ingredient?'

With a pencil stub he crossed out my entire schedule. Then, having demolished my adolescent dream structure at a single stroke, he wrote down three syllables: peace of mind.

JOSHUA LOTH LIEBMAN

Then the peace of God, which is beyond our utmost understanding, will keep guard over your hearts and your thoughts, in Christ Jesus.

And now, my friends, all that is true, all that is noble, all that is just and pure, all that is lovable and gracious, whatever is excellent and admirable—fill all your thoughts with these things.

PHILIPPIANS 4.7–8

Holy Communion

In this great healing sacrament we are supplied with all the benefits of his Passion; our spirit is cleansed by confession and absolution; our mind is fed by the ministry of the Word, and our soul and body preserved by his own Body and Blood. In our sickroom at home or in hospital when we receive our Holy Communion its reception is never in isolation, although we may be the only communicant in the household or on the ward. We come rather into the fellowship of the whole Church, militant, expectant, triumphant. It will not be 'my communion', but 'ours' in fellowship not only with Christ but with one another.

NORMAN AUTTON

Jesus replied, 'In truth, in very truth I tell you, unless you eat the flesh of the Son of Man and drink his blood you can have no life in you. Whoever eats my flesh and drinks my blood possesses eternal life, and I will raise him up on the last day. My flesh is real food; my blood is real drink. Whoever eats my flesh and drinks my blood dwells continually in me and I dwell in him.'

JOHN 6.53-6

Anointing

Anointing is a very ancient practice in the Church of God. There is nothing magical or supernatural about it, and it is not (or should not be) particularly associated with 'last rites', as so many people imagine it to be. I look upon it as a sacrament indicating the binding together of God and man. Now, in this fragment of space and time, God was binding together with himself a surgeon, a highly trained medical team, and myself. . . . 8.30 and sister and a theatre assistant wheeled my bed out of the room, down the ward . . . and into the theatre unit. . . . The blinding awareness that the Now is slipping away and that a mysterious, unknowable journey is beginning. The diminishing echo of clear-cut words in my mind: 'Jesus, come with me . . .'

JAMES DAVIDSON ROSS

Is one of you ill? He should send for the elders of the congregation to pray over him and anoint him with oil in the name of the Lord. The prayer offered in faith will save the sick man, the Lord will raise him from his bed, and any sins he may have committed will be forgiven. Therefore confess your sins to one another, and pray for one another, and then you will be healed.

JAMES 5.14–16

True Healing

What we should expect in healing is not simply a physical miracle although this is what the majority of people do expect. When people turn to their friends asking for their prayers, or to the priest for sacramental ministration, their intention is focussed on the physical side of healing. Very seldom do people say 'It does not matter whether I am healed physically, I am aware of something within me which is the root of my illness and it is this which must be healed. As to physical healing, it may follow or it may not but it will not matter.'

METROPOLITAN ANTHONY OF SOUROZH

Now there is at Jerusalem by the sheep market a pool, which is called in the Hebrew tongue Bethesda, having five porches. . . . And a certain man was there, which had an infirmity thirty and eight years. When Jesus saw him lie, and knew that he had been now a long time in that case, he saith unto him, Wilt thou be made whole?

JOHN 5.2, 5–6 A.V.

Church and Medicine

The Bishop of — leaned over me and I felt his hands lightly on my head. Quietness and healing. They swept over and through me like a flood. Despite my confusion I became aware again, this time with absolute conviction, that two factors were dragging me away from death towards life. On one hand was the constant, never-failing care of the medical staff: surgeons, doctors, sisters, nurses, physiotherapists; all backed up by the complex scientific organisation of a super-modern hospital. On the other hand, and inextricably tied to it, the strength which came to me from a non-stop outpouring of prayer from family, friends, and total strangers. Weak and muddled though I was, I knew that both factors were vital to my very life.

JAMES DAVIDSON ROSS

And while he was proclaiming the message to them, a man was brought who was paralysed. Four men were carrying him, but because of the crowd they could not get him near. So they opened up the roof over the place where Jesus was, and when they had broken through they lowered the stretcher on which the paralysed man was lying. When Jesus saw their faith, he said to the paralysed man, 'My son, your sins are forgiven. . . . I say to you, stand up, take your bed, and go home.' And he got up, and at once took his stretcher and went out in full view of them all, so that they were astounded and praised God. 'Never before', they said, 'have we seen the like.'

MARK 2.2–5, 11–12

Taking Things for Granted

I remember the first time I was taken to a camp-bed outside
after a long illness; it seemed almost literally 'heaven' to see
the blue sky flecked with white clouds overhead and to get
the sense of space after being confined to bed for so long . . .
Later, when at last able to be in a chair near the window, it
was an almost unbelievable joy just to be able to sit up
instead of having to do everything lying down. Later still,
just being able to walk round the garden on my own feet
was a greater thrill than I could have believed before my
illness. We do take so much for granted and so often only
appreciate our blessings when we have lost them.

A. GRAHAM IKIN

Acclaim the Lord, all men on earth,
worship the Lord in gladness;
enter his presence with songs of exultation.
Know that the Lord is God;
he has made us and we are his own,
his people, the flock which he shepherds.
Enter his gates with thanksgiving
and his courts with praise.
Give thanks to him and bless his name;
for the Lord is good and his love is everlasting,
his constancy endures to all generations.

PSALM 100

Convalescence

Lord, for weeks and months I have been helpless, being washed and fed, amused and spoiled, now you are beginning to give me back your gift of health. Give me courage to use your strength to take each step as I am asked, patience to be as slow as you want to be, daring to go faster than I feel I can go, and above all help me to forget myself . . . so that I may become again totally given to you through others.

MICHAEL HOLLINGS AND ETTA GULLICK

For the Spirit that God gave us is no craven spirit, but one to inspire strength, love, and self-discipline. So never be ashamed of your testimony to our Lord . . . but take your share of suffering for the sake of the Gospel, in the strength that comes from God. It is he who brought us salvation and called us to a dedicated life, not for any merit of ours but of his own purpose and his own grace, which was granted to us in Christ Jesus from all eternity.

2 TIMOTHY 1.7–9

Ending the Day

At the end of a common day's life, with all care, and no deliberate handling of unclean things, our hands are soiled. Life in this world is like that. Even our bodies, clothed and covered from contact with the outside world, are soiled. Living in the world we know inevitably brings defiling. So it is with soul and spirit. The day's living, in contact with much that is stained with evil, in the common world we know, brings its own soiling and weakening. At the close of the day, even where no deliberate sin appears, we ask for cleansing from the dust of the way, the soil of the day's life with all its contacts. And God gives it, with refreshing and renewal and rest in His gift.

GEORGE S. STEWART

If I lift up my eyes to the hills,
where shall I find help?
Help comes only from the Lord,
maker of heaven and earth.

. . .

The Lord is your guardian,
your defence at your right hand;
the sun will not strike you by day
nor the moon by night.
The Lord will guard you against all evil;
he will guard you, body and soul.
The Lord will guard your going and your coming,
now and for evermore.

PSALM 121.1-2, 5-8

At the End of Our Resources

God does not protect us against catastrophes. He is neither a lightning-rod nor a breakwater. But he comes to our aid in catastrophes. It is in the very midst of the tempest and the misfortune that a wonderful zone of peace, serenity, and joy bursts in us, if we dwell in his grace. God does not help us before we have helped ourselves. God does not relieve us before we have exhausted our own strength.

But when we are at the end of our resources, when everything is going the worst . . . at this moment he manifests himself, and we begin to know that he has been there all along.

LOUIS EVELY

God is our shelter and our refuge,
a timely help in trouble;
so we are not afraid when the earth heaves
and the mountains are hurled into the sea,
when its waters seethe in tumult
and the mountains quake before his majesty.
. . .
Let be then: learn that I am God,
high over the nations, high above earth.
The Lord of Hosts is with us,
the God of Jacob our high stronghold.

PSALM 46.1–3, 10–11

No Improvement

It may be that some who read these words are not getting better. You may have been ill a long time, and though you have prayed to be well, and sought all the help towards healing that can be given you, by the Church's ministry on the spiritual side as well as by the skill of doctors and nurses on the human side, the hope of getting back to health is very slight. Some may read these words whose weakness is growing greater, or whose infirmities are those of old age. . . . Suffering borne patiently and even joyfully is a witness to those around you of the love and power of Him whose greater glory you seek.

T. W. Crafer

Truly my heart waits silently for God;
my deliverance comes from him.
In truth he is my rock of deliverance,
my tower of strength, so that I stand unshaken.
My deliverance and my honour depend upon God,
God who is my rock of refuge and my shelter.
Trust always in God, my people,
pour out your hearts before him;
God is our shelter.

Psalm 62.1–2, 7–8

Signs of Diminishment

When the signs of age begin to mark my body (and still more when they touch my mind); when the ill that is to diminish me or carry me off strikes from without or is born within me; when the painful moment comes in which I suddenly awaken to the fact that I am ill or growing old; . . . in all those dark moments, O God, grant that I may understand that it is You (provided only my faith is strong enough) who are painfully parting the fibres of my being in order to penetrate to the very marrow of my substance and bear me away within Yourself.

PIERRE TEILHARD DE CHARDIN

. . . let us continue at peace with God through our Lord Jesus Christ, through whom we have been allowed to enter the sphere of God's grace, where we now stand. Let us exult in the hope of the divine splendour that is to be ours. More than this: let us even exult in our present sufferings, because we know that suffering trains us to endure, and endurance brings proof that we have stood the test, and this proof is the ground of hope. Such a hope is no mockery, because God's love has flooded our inmost heart through the Holy Spirit he has given us.

ROMANS 5.2–5

Letting Go

Pain is terrible, but surely you need not have fear as well?
Can you not see death as the friend and deliverer? It means
stripping off that body which is tormenting you: like taking
off a hairshirt or getting out of a dungeon. What is there to
be afraid of? . . .

Remember, tho' we struggle against things because we
are afraid of them, it is often the other way round—we get
afraid because we struggle. Are you struggling, resisting?
Don't you think Our Lord says to you 'Peace, child, peace.
Relax. Let go. Underneath are the everlasting arms. Let go,
I will catch you. Do you trust me so little?'

Of course this may not be the end. Then make it a good
rehearsal.

C. S. LEWIS

'Set your troubled hearts at rest. Trust in God always;
trust also in me. There are many dwelling-places in my
Father's house; if it were not so I should have told you;
for I am going there on purpose to prepare a place for you.
. . . Peace is my parting gift to you, my own peace, such as
the world cannot give. Set your troubled hearts at rest, and
banish your fears.'

JOHN 14.1–2, 27

Fullness of Life

We are apt to think of healing as getting rid of people's normal pain, disease, disability, distress. But healing is really restoring to the true normality, restoring to full manhood, mending the breaches in our perfect humanity, and making us again what God intends us to be. It shows us His life-giving spirit; the Lord and Giver of Life ever at work producing and restoring fullness of life. For all disease of soul or body is a subtraction from human nature, a way of being substandard . . . So, healing of any sort is a kind of creative or rather regenerating work, a direct expression and furtherance of God's Will. It means bringing life back to what it ought to be, mending that which has broken down, healing our deep mental and spiritual wounds by the action of His charity, giving new strength to the weak, new purity to the tainted.

EVELYN UNDERHILL

So shall we all at last attain to the unity inherent in our faith and our knowledge of the Son of God—to mature manhood, measured by nothing less than the full stature of Christ. . . . He is the head, and on him the whole body depends. Bonded and knit together by every constituent joint, the whole frame grows through the due activity of each part, and builds itself up in love.

EPHESIANS 4.13, 16

Wholeness

As sickness is a challenge, so is healing, for health is far more than a physical problem. Our symptoms may now have been alleviated; our disease or disorder eradicated by either medicine or surgery, our bodily functions restored, yet we are not truly healed until the spiritual side of our nature has been taken into account, and we are endeavouring to serve God with all our heart, mind and strength. No matter how sound our physical, mental and social aspects might be, without the spiritual our total picture will always be less than complete. Rather sadly we seem far more anxious to combat sickness than promote health, and consequently we have come to know more about disease than we do about healing.

NORMAN AUTTON

And now, my friends, farewell . . . take our appeal to heart; agree with one another; live in peace; and the God of love and peace will be with you. Greet one another with the kiss of peace. All God's people send you greetings.

The grace of the Lord Jesus Christ, and the love of God, and fellowship in the Holy Spirit, be with you all.

2 CORINTHIANS 13.11–14

Sources

20 IN CONTINUING PAIN   William Barclay, *Prayers for Help and Healing*. Collins Fontana 1968.

21 MENTAL PAIN   Norman W. Goodacre, *Springboard for Easter*. A. R. Mowbray 1966.

22 BEARING PAIN   *John Leonard Wilson: Confessor for the Faith*, ed. Roy McKay. Hodder & Stoughton 1973.

23 FORTITUDE   Evelyn Underhill, *Light of Christ*. Longmans 1944.

24 THE TRUE FUNCTION OF SUFFERING   As page 13.

25 THE SOUND OF SILENCE   Norton Juster, *The Phantom Tollbooth*. Collins 1962.

26 THE SILENCE OF JESUS   As page 15.

27 WHEN TIRED   As page 17.

28 SUFFERING IN CHRIST   Father Congreve, *Spiritual Letters*, ed. W. H. Longridge. A. R. Mowbray 1928.

29 THE HEALING CROSS   As page 15.

30 VICTORY THROUGH MASTERY   H. A. Williams, *The True Wilderness*. Constable 1965.

31 ONE DAY AT A TIME   J. Neville Ward, *Five for Sorrow, Ten for Joy*. Epworth Press 1971.

32 LIFT UP YOUR HEARTS   Brother Lawrence, *The Practice of the Presence of God*. Epworth Press 1968.

33 JOY IN ADVERSITY   Hugh Lavery in the *Daily Telegraph* 1975.

34 HELPING OTHERS   G. E. Childs, *A Parson's Thoughts on Pain*. A. R. Mowbray 1949.

35 INNER STRENGTH   Rabindranath Tagore, *Collected Poems and Plays*. Macmillan 1936.

36 SUPERNATURAL STRENGTH   Ruth Pitter in *Pause for Thought*, ed. Joanna Scott-Moncrieff. B.B.C. Publications 1971.

37 BEING RECEPTIVE   A patient's letter to Jung in *The Secret of the Golden Flower*, tr. R. Wilhelm, Commentary by C. G. Jung, English tr. C. F. Baynes. Routledge & Kegan Paul 1965.

38 THE LOVE OF GOD   *The Silver Lining*, ed. Richard Tatlock. Bodley Head 1954.

39 WE SHALL OVERCOME   W. R. Matthews, *Christian Meditations*, published by the *Daily Telegraph* 1973.

40 CONTENTMENT   Metropolitan Anthony of Sourozh (after Martin Buber), *The Churches' Council for Health and Healing*, Bulletin No. 3, 1968.

41 INNER GROWTH   T. W. Crafer, *The Church's Help in Sickness*. S.P.C.K. 1937.

42 WILLING ACCEPTANCE   Leonard Wilson in *The Burrswood Herald* 1964.

43 THE CHRISTIAN COMMUNITY   George Appleton, *Journey for a Soul*. Collins 1974.

44 MEMBERS OF A FAMILY   Gerald Vann, *The Pain of Christ*. Blackfriars 1947.

45 LONELINESS   Hugh Montefiore, *Truth to Tell*. Collins 1966.

46 MORE THAN CONQUERORS   Francis Paget, *The Spirit of Discipline*. Longmans 1903.

47 THE GRACE OF GRATITUDE   As page 14.

48 THANK YOU, LORD   As page 12.

49 LOSING FAITH   As page 14.

50 A SENSE OF HUMOUR   E. R. Morgan (ed.), *Reginald Somerset Ward: His Life and Letters*. A. R. Mowbray 1963.

51 THE PRESENT MOMENT   As page 9.

52 STRENGTH IN WEAKNESS   Elizabeth Bassett, *Love is My Meaning*. Darton, Longman & Todd 1975.

53 WAITING . . . WAITING   C. S. Lewis, *Letters to Malcolm*. Collins Fontana 1966.

54 PATIENCE   As page 17.

55 BEFORE AN OPERATION   Norman Autton, *When Sickness Comes*. Church in Wales Publications 1973.

56 PENITENCE   As page 18.

57 PEACE OF MIND   Joshua Loth Liebman, *Peace of Mind*. Heinemann 1946.

58 HOLY COMMUNION   As page 55.

59 ANOINTING   James Davidson Ross, *The Heart Machine*. Hodder Paperbacks 1973. (First published by A. R. Mowbray.)

60 TRUE HEALING   As page 40.

61 CHURCH AND MEDICINE   As page 59.

62 TAKING THINGS FOR GRANTED   A. Graham Ikin, *Live and Learn*. Epworth Press 1955.

63 CONVALESCENCE   As page 12.

64 ENDING THE DAY   As page 3.

65 AT THE END OF OUR RESOURCES   Louis Evely, *Joy and Suffering*. Search Press 1967.

66 NO IMPROVEMENT   As page 41.

67 SIGNS OF DIMINISHMENT   Pierre Teilhard de Chardin, *Le Milieu Divin*. Collins Fontana 1969.

68 LETTING GO   C. S. Lewis, *Letters to an American Lady*. Hodder & Stoughton 1969.

69 FULLNESS OF LIFE   As page 23.

70 WHOLENESS   As page 55.

Index of Authors

Index of Scriptural Readings